Animals in the Wild

Tiger

by Mary Hoffman

62489

Raintree Childrens Books
Milwaukee
Belitha Press Limited • London

When tigers are cubs, they are playful. They look like other cats. But the cubs become very large adult tigers.

Tigers are the biggest of all the big cats. A tiger is one of the most feared animals in the wild. And it is one of the strongest, too.

Newborn cubs are small, blind, and helpless. Their mother cares for them by herself. Two or more cubs are born at a time.

Cubs are able to see well by the time they
are three weeks old. At six weeks old, they
go with their mother when she hunts.

The tiger mother shows her cubs how to hunt. They watch from a hiding place. The mother will not have more cubs until the ones that she has are able to hunt alone.

Hunting is very important. Tigers hunt for the food that they need to keep alive. At first, the mother kills animals for herself and her cubs. Then the cubs hunt, too.

The cubs stay with their mother for about
two years. Then they're on their own. Each
tiger finds its own territory. A tiger's territory
is between 25 and 250 square miles.

In its territory, a tiger needs enough large animals to keep it alive. Tigers also need water and shade. They can live in a warm place or a cold place.

All tigers have stripes. Some rare tigers
have coats that are white with black
stripes. Most tigers are orange with black
stripes or a pale color with brown stripes.

Tigers have sharp eyes. They can also hear
well, and they use their sense of smell
when hunting. Their powerful teeth and
jaws easily tear apart prey that they catch.

A tiger can hide well in the shade of trees.
Its stripes and its color make a tiger
difficult to see in the spots of light.

Tigers also hide well in long grass. They sleep during the day and hunt at night. Tigers begin stalking prey by waiting.

When prey passes by, a tiger leaps and runs to catch it. Tigers only run fast for a short time, so their timing must be just right.

Tigers hunt large animals, like deer and
wild pigs. They catch about thirty a year.
But hungry tigers will even eat birds.

Tigers weigh 300 to more than 400
pounds. They can eat fifty pounds of food
at a sitting, and they drink a lot of water.

Tigers cool off by swimming. They have to
watch out for crocodiles. A crocodile can
pull a tiger underwater and drown it.

Some people in India try to protect
living tigers. Most of the tigers have

been killed. Even the biggest of the
big cats needs protection.

First published in this edition in the United States of America 1984
by Raintree Publishers Inc., 310 West Wisconsin Avenue,
Milwaukee, Wisconsin 53203.

Library of Congress Number: 84-15120

First published in the United Kingdom under the title
Animals in the Wild—Tiger
by Windward, an imprint owned by W H Smith Ltd., St. John's
House, East Street, Leicester LE1 6NE, by arrangement with
Belitha Press Ltd.

Text and illustrations in this form © Belitha Press 1983
Text © Mary Hoffman 1983

Dedicated to Phyllis Hoffman

Scientific Adviser: Dr. Gwynne Vevers
Picture Researcher: Stella Martin
Designer: Julian Holland

Acknowledgements are due to Bruce Coleman Ltd
for all photographs in this book with the following
exceptions: Jacana Ltd. Cover, pp 4, 11; Eric Hosking p 14;
Natural History Photographic Agency pp 8-9

ISBN 0-8172-2405-X (U.S.A.)

Library of Congress Cataloging in Publication Data

Hoffman, Mary, 1945—
     Tiger.

     (Animals in the wild)
     Summary: Shows the tiger in its natural
surroundings and describes its life and struggle
for survival.
     1. Tigers—Juvenile literature [1. Tigers]
I. Title. II. Series.
QL737.C22H6   1984   599.74′428   84-15120
ISBN 0-8172-2405-X

2 3 4 5 6 7 8 9   89 88 87 86